Santa Muerte

The History and Rituals of
the Mexican Folk Saint

Table of Contents

Introduction

What makes a saint? For some people, it's how a person carried themselves in life and their impact on others. For others, it's their spiritual connection to God. Yet, even among the most venerated, some were never canonized and never acquired the title of saint. We call them folk saints – dead people and indigenous spirits that were never truly acknowledged as saints. This, however, has never stopped their devotees from believing that they are intercessors with God in the same way that canonized saints are.

Why then have those folk saints not been canonized? Because many of them went against the current, acted upon their conscience, and followed their hearts. For that, they were labeled sinners and false idols. In the eyes of their followers, though, they were much more. They were healers, folk heroes, and indigenous spirits worthy of the veneration of being saints. Perhaps what makes folk saints so popular is how relatable they are to the members of their communities, with most of them originating from the same places as their followers. This is why, in death, they remain a significant and active part of many people's lives.

One of the most popular folk saints in Latin America, particularly in Mexico, is Santa Muerte, shortened from Nuestra Señora de la Santa Muerte, which translates to 'Our Lady of the Holy Death.' As you can probably already tell, Santa Muerte is no ordinary folk saint. It's the personification of death itself. It may seem odd that a group of people would venerate death, but this has been practiced for centuries. We'll get to that in just a bit.

Santa Muerte is more than simply a personification of death. A female deity, she is associated with a lot of good by her followers. Santa Muerte is responsible for protection, healing, and safe passage to the afterlife for those who venerated her in life. This deity has significantly grown in popularity over the past few decades, much to the dismay of the Catholic Church, Mexican government, and other official bodies.

You can see her now in many places in Mexico with shrines erected in her name and the many followers associated with the Santa Muerte movement or cult.

While she was originally a male figure, Santa Muerte is now almost exclusively female in most places you find her. She's a skeletal figure dressed in a long robe with a globe or a scythe in her hands. The colors she adorns can vary from one devotee to another, so there are no limitations to what she can wear. Santa Muerte has many other names like the Bony Lady, the White Girl, the Godmother, the Skinny One, and the Most Holy Death. She is revered by millions across the Americas, with the majority of her followers originating in Mexico.

Why then is Santa Muerte this popular? In many ways, she is the beloved saint and patron of the dispossessed - those who have lost everything. Santa Muerte has often been depicted in popular culture, especially in movies and TV, as being associated with criminals and drug cartels, but she is so much more than that stereotypical depiction to many people. For her devotees, Santa Muerte is a non-judgmental, benevolent deity. She is believed to have the ability to grant the wishes of those who offer her pledges or offerings. For that reason, some scholars like Andrew Chesnut, professor of Latin American history and author of a book on her, believe that the followers of the Santa Muerte make for the fastest-growing religion in the world, with at least 10 million followers worldwide.

In this book, we will explore the story of Santa Muerte and how she came to be the cult symbol and folk saint that she is today. We will discuss the influences of folk Catholicism on Santa Muerte and how many of her followers drew upon traditional religions to establish their own. We will also explore the practices of Santa Muerte followers and their shrines for the Lady of the Holy Death.

Chapter One:

Death as a Deity

People worshiping death figures or deities is not new, and it existed long before Santa Muerte. From Hecate and Hades in Greek mythology to Anubis in ancient Egyptian mythology, civilizations have revered death for thousands of years. Santa Muerte is another in a long line of deities personifying death. According to some scholars, the most accurate translation is "Saint Death," which is a more relevant way to describe her as opposed to 'Holy Death.' This also shows the identity and place of Santa Muerte for many as a folk saint rather than merely death. In some rituals, she is referred to as Santisima Muerte, which translates to 'Most Saintly Death,' another peeve of evidence pointing to the venerated place she occupies in her devotees' lives. So, when has Santa Muerte appeared to affect many lives? While she has gained exponential popularity over the past couple of decades, she has actually been around for centuries.

To trace the origins of Santisima Muerte, we have to go back in time to the Spanish conquest of the Aztec. True to the spirit of such conquests, the Spaniards attempted to convert the Aztec to Catholicism in the same way they did the Mayans and other civilizations conquered during those times. Naturally, there was resistance by the natives to embrace a new religion. The Spaniards tried to thwart that resistance by introducing the female grim reaper as an embodiment of death, but the locals already worshiped death in the form of male and female deities.

Mictlantecuhtli was the Aztec God of death who ruled the underworld with his wife, the Goddess Mictecacíhuatl. In Aztec culture, those who died by drowning, childbirth, war, and some diseases had to make a four-year journey in the afterlife and go through arduous trials in the nine hells of the underworld (Mictlan). In the last hell, Mictlantecuhtli lived. Those weary souls would only find rest when they got there, and they would disappear and find rest after overcoming the trials.

Mictecacíhuatl was quite literally known as the 'Lady of the Dead' and is the first citing of such a deity long before Santa Muerte. Her role was to preside over the festivals honoring the dead. She also guarded the bones of the dead. Today, some festivals date back to her, like Día de los Muertos, or day of the dead, which is a traditional Mexican festival held every year from October 31st to November 2nd. This is a practice that is derived from the Aztec civilization. The Catholic church even commemorated a celebration of its own, thereby observing its importance for the peoples of Latin American – All Souls Day, held on November 1st and 2nd. This was obviously done at a more tolerant time.

While much lore can be found about Mictlantecuhtli, there are fewer stories on his wife, the Lady of the Dead Mictecacíhuatl. Some tales say that she was sacrificed as an infant, not long after she was born, and then grew to become the Lady of the Dead. Together with her husband, they had power over the three types of souls that ended up in the underworld: those with heroic deaths, those with non-heroic deaths, and those with normal deaths.

The myth surrounding them has many variations, each carrying an interesting tale. Some say that Mictlantecuhtli and Mictecacíhuatl had a role in creating new species as they collected the bones of the dead and returned them to the land of the living so that they could be restored and create new life. Most importantly, though, is Mictecacíhuatl's earlier representation in ancient cultures, which was in the form of a skeleton or a de-fleshed body. For the Aztec, Mictecacíhuatl had a skull for a face and saggy breasts, and she wore a skirt of serpents.

In the early 1500s, the Spaniards conquered the Aztecs, and traditional religious beliefs were forced to remain hidden. In the 1700s, the Spanish documented worship and veneration of the Lady of the Dead, though they couldn't find many of her followers. It took a few more centuries until the 1900s for Santa Muerte to make a comeback and enter many people's lives. During those years, there was little mention of Santa Muerte except in some official documents or by some historians.

The evolution of Santa Muerte is fascinating to behold as some believe it is the result of mixing religions and cultural traditions. While the Spaniards conquered many countries and tried to force the spread of Catholicism, they were also smart about it. They didn't always uproot the existing religious beliefs but rather tried to blend with them, which is most likely what gave birth to Santa Muerte. She holds a scythe in some modern depictions, which shouldn't be surprising considering that her original inspiration was Mictecacíhuatl, goddess of the underworld.

A few other scholars and followers have different theories as to the origins of Santa Muerte. They believe that Santa Muerte originated from the Yoruba traditions that were carried to the Caribbean by African slaves, not much unlike Cuban Santería or Haitian Vodou. One of the myths supporting this claim comes from an urban legend claiming Santa Muerte herself appeared before a healer in Veracruz in the nineteenth century. Veracruz is a Mexican state that has the most notable and ingrained Caribbean traditions in the country.

Symbolism

As mentioned earlier, saints are those who have died and were canonized by the Catholic Church. This, however, has not been the case for Santa

Muerte. She is considered more of a folk saint who is believed to be holy due to her miracle work. However, it must be noted that Santa Muerte is not like an ordinary saint–someone who died and whose spirit is revered. She is not a dead human being but rather the personification of death itself. For many of her followers, Santa Muerte symbolizes a supernatural version of themselves, which is why she is revered as a folk saint. She is considered to be of the same social class and nationality, a symbol of their struggles and pains.

Some have even symbolized her scythe as a powerful weapon that destroys divisions based on gender, race, and social class. Her followers claim that the Bony Lady doesn't judge or discriminate, which is one of the reasons why many love her. She is associated with a safe path after death and protection and spiritual healing and financial well-being. The beauty of the Santa Muerte is that she is whatever her devotees want her to be, which is why many hold her in higher regard than other saints and religious figures. She is not just the goddess of death but also a hard-working folk saint who punishes the unjust and heals and provides for those in need. She is everything her followers need her to be.

To dive deeper into the symbolism associated with Santa Muerte, let's examine her depiction. She is often shown to hold a globe and a scythe. As we mentioned just earlier, the scythe symbolizes her protection and dominion over the dead. For many, it also symbolizes the cutting of dark energies and evil influences. The scythe is also a tool for harvesting, so it can symbolize prosperity and hope, which is representative of harvests. As for the globe, it encompasses everywhere on the mortal plane, which illustrates death's vast domain as well as its dominion over the earth. The scythe's long handle is also sometimes used to symbolize lady death's long reach.

Other items are sometimes associated with Santa Muerte. Scales are occasionally seen as one of her objects, a symbol of justice and impartiality. Scales have been a symbol of the divine will for a very long time. Santa Muerte is sometimes seen holding an hourglass, a symbol that death is not the end. When you invert the hourglass, you start over. It also goes to show her connection to time across different planes, mortal and non-mortal. An hourglass is also a symbol of patience, one of Santa Muerte's many virtues.

You can sometimes see Santa Muerte with a lamp that she uses to light the darkness and guide her followers through ignorance, hate, and doubt. A lamp is also a symbol of intelligence and strong willpower. Then there's the owl, which is associated with Mictlantecuhtli and other death deities and symbolizes wisdom. The owl has been used as a symbol and messenger of death deities for centuries and is also evidence that Santa Muerte is the continuation of these deities today. However, some believe that Santa Muerte stands above others and should not be compared to former or present death deities. A few devotees even believe she will punish those who dare put her picture or statue next to other deities.

There have been varying depictions of Santa Muerte over the years, with artists taking creative liberties in displaying what she means to them. Some depictions, however, have been so controversial that even the prominent figures of the Santa Muerte movement in Mexico have advised against using them. An example is an artist combining the image of Santa Muerte with the Virgin of Guadalupe, stirring a lot of controversy in all sects. The Catholic Church considered it an outrage and condemned this depiction. On the other hand, many Santa Muerte followers also found it to be offensive since it weakened the image of their powerful folk saint, the Most Holy Death, as it compared her with a separate female entity that symbolizes pain and suffering rather than strength and dominance.

Lingering in the Shadows

It is believed that Santa Muerte remained secret for many years. The first documented mention of her in veneration was in Mexico in 1797 in a Spanish Inquisition report. This is over 200 years after the Spanish conquest of the Aztec. Throughout that time, many still worshiped Santa Muerte and believed in her, whether in her old form as Mictecacíhuatl or in its modern form, but they didn't really come out of the shadows for a very long time. The worship of death in the Aztec territories waned over the years after the Spanish conquest, but it was never really eliminated entirely.

Over the years, it made sense that the Santa Muerte symbol would evolve from a male figure into a female one, considering that Mexicans have an affinity towards female symbols. The people there have always been fond of the Virgin of Guadalupe, who has a more significant cult following than any other Catholic saint. It made sense that a female character symbolized the Mexican symbol of death.

Over the years, there have been a few mentions of Santa Muerte in written text, scarce as it has been. It wasn't until the 90s that she became a folk saint and hero in the eyes of millions, and it happened on account of a wave of violence that swept across Mexico during the drug wars.

Chapter Two:

Santa Muerte in the Modern World

The Day of the Dead is a Mexican tradition that pre-dated the Spanish conquest, and it remained present throughout the campaign and long after, even to this very day. It has been a long-standing tradition in the country and the most popular celebration of the dead. For Mexicans, the Day of the Dead is when they celebrate the dead and invite them to return among the living. It's an ode to the life they once lived by those they have left behind. This tradition pre-dates Santa Muerte when there was a strong death cult in Mexico where altars were set up for the deceased, and people would chant, dance, and listen to music.

Despite this prevailing veneration and admiration for the dead, Santa Muerte was not openly celebrated for a long time, even during enduring holidays such as the Day of the Dead.

However, before her veneration grew in the late twentieth century, there was documentation of Santa Muerte in Mexico in 1940. It shouldn't come as a surprise that this was mostly among working-class neighborhoods in Mexico City like Tepito. The people residing in these poorer parts believed in her and revered Santa Muerte.

Over the next few decades, her presence grew in smaller circles, but in the height of the drug wars in the 1990s, Santa Muerte turned from an occult fascination to a public hero and many saw her as a protaginist. The lives of the Mexican people grew more complicated during the 1980s and 1990s with the rise of violence and the spread of drug trafficking. Society wasn't kind to its lower classes, and a lot of Mexicans lived in abject poverty. Many looked for a savior to snatch them from that suffering, and some found it in Santa Muerte.

One of the most famous incidents in which the cult of Santa Muerte came under the spotlight was in 1998 when the police arrested a man called Daniel Arizmendi López, a gangster associated with notorious criminal activities. When the police apprehended him, a shrine to Santa Muerte was discovered in his home. Naturally, the press extensively covered this, and associations between Santa Muerte and violence began developing. Other notorious drug traffickers with shrines dedicated to Santa Muerte in their homes during that time, which only fueled the speculation about her connection to criminality.

Yet, in a strange paradox, Santa Muerte was more than a patroness for the drug lords and gangsters during those violent times. She was also a revered symbol for many of the policemen who hunted them. Santa Muerte was as much a guardian angel for the criminals of the underworld as she was a symbol of the drug war, revered and respected on both sides. Over the following few decades, Santa Muerte's popularity saw a meteoric rise, with shrines being erect to her all across the county.

She was loved and revered by not just criminals, outlaws, and the cops. She was loved by those living on the fringes of society, and she remains quite popular among them to this very day. Andrew Chesnut estimates that most Mexicans didn't even know of Santa Muerte by 2001. "She was unknown to 99 percent of Mexicans before 2001 when she went public. Now I estimate there are some 10-12 million devotees, mostly in Mexico, but also significant numbers in the United States and Central America," he explains.

Santa Muerte moved from being only mentioned to invoke love miracles in the period between the 1940s and 1980s to being the patron saint of the fastest-growing religious movement in the world. In 2001, the first modern shrine for Santa Muerte was created in Mexico City in none other than Tepito, where a lot of workers had already been cited revering Santa Muerte in the early 1900s. This was the first openly created shrine for her, and it saw the beginning of the spread of devotion for Santa Muerte in Mexico and beyond.

As the intensity of the drug wars grew, more people embraced Santa Muerte as their savior. It didn't matter if you were a security guard or drug lord. Many felt that death was always right around the corner, and they could use all the protection and help they could get. Some priests and religious experts believe that Santa Muerte was popular among hardened criminals because even they had Catholicism ingrained into every part of their lives. These criminals didn't feel easy about asking God or any other Catholic saint for help with their criminal activities. This is where Santa Muerte came in. She was a folk saint and a revered deity that they could pray to and ask for help in their crimes without shame. This is in keeping with the previously mentioned characteristic of being non-judgmental, for which Santa Muerte is best known.

The Following

Since 2001, people began proudly displaying their Santa Muerte statues and effigies outside their homes, restaurants, and workplaces. Doña Queta was one of the people who played a huge role in attracting many to the cult of Santa Muerte. In 2001, she was working as a quesadilla seller. She put a Santa Muerte effigy, life-size, outside her home in Tepito. Without planning it, her shrine became the most popular of Santa Muerte's cult in all of Mexico, attracting followers and devotees in large numbers over the following ten years. It wouldn't be an overstatement to say that Doña Queta played the most important role in transforming the veneration of Santa Muerte in modern-day Mexico and converting her following into a public and popular cult.

Not far from Queta, also in Tepito, David Romo established the first Santa Muerte church in the late 2000s. He declared himself the Archbishop, and his church borrowed much from Roman Catholic doctrine. We will explore some of the similarities between Catholicism and the Santa Muerte doctrine in a bit. But the church still separated itself from the Catholic Church, even after borrowing many liturgies and holding everything from masses to weddings. However, the Traditionalist Mexican-American Catholic Church hasn't been active since 2011 after the arrest of David Romo.

In the US, on the other hand, there is the Templo Santa Muerte in Los Angeles, which also offers many religious services similar to the Catholic Church like rosaries, baptism, and weddings. The founders of the church immigrated from Mexico to the US, and one of them claims to have been trained in Mexico at the hands of a shaman who supposedly taught him to speak directly with the Santa Muerte herself. There's also the Saint Death

Universal Sanctuary (Santuario Universal de Santa Muerte) not far from this church, right at the heart of LA's Mexican American community.

Santa Muerte's devotees come from every background and follow different paths. She has followers from every walk of life, from students and young kids to doctors, lawyers, politicians, artists, and criminals. There is something about Santa Muerte that is appealing to these different groups of people, and they have all found something that they're looking for in Santa Muerte. Mexico, in general, has an average young life of around 24 or 25. It shouldn't come as a surprise then that many of Santa Muerte's followers are teens and youth in their twenties and thirties. It's quite likely that there are many more people embracing Santa Muerte than official counts indicate, but we'll never know since the Catholic Church publicly condemns her. This we'll get to in a bit. Due to that tense relation between the folk saint and the Catholic Church, many people prefer to keep their devotion to Santa Muerte a private matter shared only with the closest of friends and family members.

Still, even with many keeping their faith a secret, devotion and veneration of Santa Muerte can be seen all across Mexico. You just need to walk into a random shop or market in Mexico, and you'll see no other religious figure on stalls more than the Santa Muerte. She occupies space on stalls and floors freely in any place selling religious artifacts across the country. For a couple of dollars, you can get your hands on some votive candles, the most popular of Santa Muerte products. These candles may be cheap, but they give devotees a chance to thank or invoke Santa Muerte's presence easily and directly.

Even in the streets, you'll find vendors selling figurines of Santa Muerte, especially to drivers crossing the borders to the US. Despite the Virgin of Guadalupe's immense popularity in the country, Santa Muerte figurines and products have been outselling her for the past couple of decades. The Bony Lady has been successfully crossing the US-Mexico border for some time now, which is why you shouldn't be surprised if you stumble upon her quite a few times in US cities, especially those closest to the border. Towns like El Paso, Laredo, and Brownsville have a strong Santa Muerte following. However, Santa Muerte has traveled far beyond just the border towns and delved deep into the United States.

Santa Muerte means so much to Mexicans, especially those who are trying to make the perilous journey across the borders into the US, that they have a specific prayer for her to help guide and protect them on this journey:

Most Holy Spirit of Death, I invoke your holy name to ask that you help me in this endeavor. Lead me over mountains, valleys, and paths. Don't stop showering me with your good fortune. Make sure that my destination is freed of all evil purposes. Santa Muerte, through your powerful protection, prevents problems from materializing and weighing heavily on my heart. My lady, prevent sickness from touching me and keep away tragedy, pain, and want. I light this candle so that the gleam of your eyes forms an invisible shield around me. Grant me prudence, patience, and, Holy Queen of Darkness, grant me strength, power, and wisdom. Tell the elements not to unleash their fury wherever I go. Make sure I have a happy return trip because

I'm ready to adorn and decorate your home at my holy altar.

Many Mexican Santa Muerte devotees chant this prayer as they embark on the journey to the 'other side' across the borders. They may light a gold votive candle on the eve of their trip, as recommended by the Santa Muerte bible.

Once on the other side, the immigrants still invoke the Bony Lady to help guide them in this new land and fill their lives with fortunes. You can find a significant following in many cities such as Houston, New York, Phoenix, and obviously LA due to their large Mexican and Central American populations. In US prisons, though, you will probably find the largest Santa Muerte following in the country, especially Texan and Californian prisons. In Mexico, it's pretty much the same, with the Most Holy Death being a subject of great devotion and affection for many of the inmates. In many ways, she is the saint and protector of those forced into the penal system across the US and Mexico. Despite being most popular in Mexico, many shrines are erected to Santa Muerte in the United States.

It's fascinating to behold the sway that Santa Muerte has over many people. In many ways, she is a divine figure of action with unlimited control over life and death. Her reputation is unlike any other saint, folk or otherwise. The Bony Lady acts fast and is all-powerful. She gets things done. This is why many of her followers are people who focus greatly on results and those to whom patience is not a virtue. To them, Santa Muerte is a cut above any biblical figure, saints or otherwise. Some even believe that she takes orders from God directly and answers to no one else. To many of her devotees, believing in Santa Muerte doesn't conflict with their belief in God. If anything, it makes the latter stronger, and they trust in her as God's saint and the one who fulfills his desires when it comes to life and death.

Santa Muerte for the LGBTQ

True to her acceptance of those who are rejected by society and are sometimes shunned, Santa Muerte has been a significant savior and patron of the LGBTQ communities. You could see her images and sculptures in many homes of migrant transgender sex workers living in the US, and many such communities in Mexico also venerate her. Santa Muerte has always been associated with living on the edge of the law, doing dangerous things, or simply participating in things out of the ordinary. This is why many lesbian, gay, and transgender communities have found in her a non-judgmental saint and patron who wouldn't condemn or judge them for their sexual orientation.

This is possibly another reason why the Church has often had issues with Santa Muerte, in much the same way that governments have. Despite the many disagreements between the Catholic Church and US governments, there has often been an unspoken agreement regarding policing and stifling LGBTQ communities. If you think about it, sexuality and immigration are often connected, which is why governments and the Church have often found an enemy in Santa Muerte.Strict immigration policies have always been a cornerstone of nationalist ideologies, and heteronormative practices are also in the vein of nationalism and procreation for the country it promotes. In other words, some countries are quite protective of their moral codes, which might affect their nationalist ideals.

You don't need to look past earlier legislation to see how deeply this runs. An example of radical ideologies like these is the Page Act of 1875, the first federal restrictive law in the United States. It simply stated that those entering the country for 'lewd and immoral purposes' from "China, Japan, or any oriental country" were to be banned. You'll also notice that other laws put much emphasis on 'family' in their traditional heteronormative definition. The 1965 Immigration Act gave 74% of all visas to family members to preserve the traditional notions of family thatare promoted by nationalist ideologies. Immigration laws view sexuality as a threat, especially women's, which is why there is an emphasis on the notions of a family in its most basic definition.

This kind of rhetoric was prevalent against Latino women, most of all, whose fertility scared not just the state but even society itself. There were even video games where you'd have to stop a 'breeder' -- a pregnant Latino woman -- from entering the country. This and border policies and officials have all contributed to making LGBTQ migrants, most of all, feel unwelcomed and threatened. They were treated as outcasts and rejected, feared, and hated at the same time. They were also mistreated on countless occasions. Sexual assault and rape crimes committed by border patrol agents have often been much higher than any recorded cases by officers in various other law enforcement agencies.

There are many more recorded cases of laws and amendments to immigration laws that systematically excluded LGBTQ members from entering the US. In some cases, it was flat out stated that gay and lesbian women were not to enter the country and were labeled as "sexual deviates." In the 1990s, Congress removed the provisions stopping "sexual deviants" from entering the country, but that never really stopped many LGBTQ immigrants from feeling rejected and hated. It is undeniable that nationalism was viewed in heterosexual terms most of the time, and consequently, so was immigration. This led to many Mexican and Central American immigrants feeling rejected by the country that was supposed to embrace them.

This background gives you an idea as to why Santa Muerte was extremely popular among these communities. Most migrant LGBTQ members traveling from Mexico to the US came from Catholic backgrounds, so they were already accustomed to feeling immense guilt and a sense of shame just because of their sexual preferences. Some were also forced to feel that they were not worthy of being present during religious service or ceremonies, which is a terrible experience for someone who grew up with a deeply religious background. Many migrant Mexicans within the LGBTQ community were cornered into a place of rejection, which is where Santa Muerte came in.

Those who felt like outcasts had to look for help, protection, and spiritual guidance from unlikely sources. Unofficial saints and folk heroes that were not recognized by the Church, like Santa Muerte, shared in their struggle and reflected their strange and unusual place in society. The people, especially women, of LGBTQ communities didn't really care what the origins of Santa Muerte were. They cared about her presence in their lives and how she helped them. They believed that she protected them from death and evil, despite being Lady Death herself. LGBTQ sex workers, in particular, developed a great devotion and affinity towards Santa Muerte, who adds just enough death into their lives to ward it off.

For many LGBTQ devotees, one thing that distinguishes Santa Muerte from other folk saints and deities is that she had both a male and female shape at some point, which makes her follow more inclusive and her cult more accepting of people across every gender. Just because her current form is female doesn't mean that Santa Muerte isn't accepting of males and those who don't identify as either female or male. As mentioned earlier, she doesn't care what your gender is, and she doesn't judge you for characteristics such as your sexuality. This is why she is so popular and loved within the LGBTQ communities. She's a symbol and serves as proof that they are not alone and that they can still worship and have faith without adhering to heteronormative practices.

A Saint for Those in Crisis

Adding to the previous point, it wouldn't be surprising to find out that more women than men follow Santa Muerte and are part of her cult.

In poorer communities, women are often more marginalized and mistreated. Additionally, when it comes to immigration and control over LGBTQ migrant bodies, women have always been the more targeted since they give birth and are therefore viewed as a threat to a country's national identity.

Poorer and marginalized individuals, those excluded from society and market economy, not to mention those who are not treated fairly by judicial systems and shunned out from the educational institution, have always been the majority of Santa Muerte's followers. This is most often the case in rural communities and inner cities. Some scholars label the devotion to Santa Muerte as a 'cult of crisis,' which develops during times of social and economic hardships. These hardships almost always mainly target the working class. This is why in the 1940s when Santa Muerte was still worshiped in secret, those who were still devoted to her were marginalized workers. Even after the resurgence of her popularity and the spread of dedicated shrines, it was mostly the working class and those in social and/or economic crises that flocked to Santa Muerte and invoked her name.

Despite public perception that Santa Muerte is often associated with hardened criminals, many of those convicted of crimes and follow her are just desperate people who were driven to small, petty crimes like petty theft and prostitution out of need. They are desperate for money, so they break the law out of that desperation. However, Santa Muerte occasionally attracts a few among the middle class and those with a spiritual rather than economic crisis.

A good deal of Santa Muerte's followers is those who are disillusioned with the Catholic Church and its institutional approach to their life struggles, as well as the inability of canonized saints to help them lead better lives. Those people have all but created a new religion that is a reflection of their reality of pain, discrimination, poverty, and daily struggles. The cult of Santa Muerte also reflects the uniqueness of the identities of the people in it and their nonconformity to society's standards and norms.

As mentioned earlier, a good deal of Santa Muerte's followers are not just hardened criminals and outlaws but cops and military forces who ask for her blessing when they are about to go risk their lives. Santa Muerte to them is something different but equally important and powerful. You can say that Santa Muerte is a folk saint for people in crisis who have no one else to turn to, those who have had their traditional faith fail them, and those who are let down by the norms of society and religion. She is a saint for all those people and anyone else who would embrace her as a savior and protector, regardless of their class, gender, creed, or color.

Chapter Three:

The Persecution of Santa Muerte

As you can probably imagine, a new religion rising at this meteoric rate would not have gone unnoticed. Santa Muerte's devotees were faced with a myriad of challenges and obstacles from institutions that wished to stifle the devotion and reverence that she had so quickly garnered. The Catholic Church has repeatedly denounced and attacked the Santa Muerte following and the saint herself. Moreover, the Mexican State has targeted its following on several occasions, sometimes demolishing shrines in the process. Many people of power viewed Santa Muerte as a threat, and they targeted her for that reason.

The Church

The Church never took kindly to Santa Muerte, drawing followers who were fed up with the traditional church and its inability to fix their problems or answer their prayers. The Church's stance on Santa Muerte was put under the spotlight when the Pope himself made a statement during a visit to Mexico that targeted Santa Muerte and her followers. Pope Francis gave a speech to Mexican bishops. In it, he claimed that he was "particularly concerned about those many persons who, seduced by the empty power of the world, praise illusions and embrace their macabre symbols to commemorate death in exchange for money."

For most people aware of Santa Muerte's cult, this reference was loud and clear. It was also not surprising. Santa Muerte simply challenged the authority and influence of the church, and that was not something that the Catholic Church could accept. Perhaps one of the reasons why the Church had never come to accept the Santa Muerte following was the fact that this cult and its teachings have much in common with Catholicism and have drawn much influence from it, from devotional prayers to votive candles and many other rituals.

The truth is many people who embrace Santa Muerte still consider themselves to be good Catholics, which is the real challenge for the Church. Many find no contradictions between worshipping Santa Muerte and being Catholics, which the Church has always found to be problematic. Another reason why the Church has a problem with the Bony Lady is that she is said to grant any favor or request free of judgment, which has obviously never been a trait of the Catholic Church or something that it preaches.

The Church's dismay at the Santa Muerte reverence is not modern, though it has increased with the rise of the Bony Lady's popularity among many Catholics. The Church became aware of Santa Muerte's devotees in the 18th century, and it acted on that knowledge and destroyed any Santa Muerte shrines erect by the indigenous people.

For the Church, Santa Muerte is a false idol, which is why opposition to it has been around for this long. "Worship of Saint Death is a grave error, and if any man, woman or Catholic continues this, it will be through ignorance or because they already left the Catholic faith," said José Luis Chávez Botello, Archbishop of Oaxaca, one of the places with many Santa Muerte devotees. There is a contradiction between being a faithful practitioner and a devotee to Santa Muerte for the

Catholic Church. Many of its pastors and priests find the Bony Lady to be an abomination: a saint who will accept any offerings even if they were cigarettes and alcohol, a protector who will watch over the criminals and the sinners and grant favors to all those who would ask.

Tensions between the Church and the cult of Santa Muerte have risen over the past few decades, escalating to great proportions at times. At one point, the Church declared the worship of Santa Muerte to be a satanic practice and its followers a satanic cult. This happened in response to some Catholics separating from the church and trying to capture some Catholic buildings. This powerful condemnation came as a surprise to many who viewed it as a targeted attack on Santa Muerte and her followers rather than just opposing views between different faiths. This directly contradicted the fact that many of the Santa Muerte devotees considered themselves Catholics. At another point, Cardinal Gianfranco Ravasi, the head of the Vatican's Pontifical Council for Culture, described the Santa Muerte cult and worship as a "degeneration of religion."

This hostility toward Santa Muerte has often been surprising to many of her devotees who consider themselves to still be part of Catholicism. While some may have strayed off, many still view Santa Muerte in light of Catholic practices rather than being a separate entity or religion of her own. You can find many paintings in Santa Muerte's church in Puebla depicting the Bony Lady seated with Jesus. Some Santa Muerte followers believe she welcomed Jesus into the world of the dead, which further illustrates the connection between Santa Muerte and Catholicism. You can also find churches of Santa Muerte in Mexico organizing trips all the time to the Basilica of Our Lady of Guadalupe in Mexico City, one of the most venerated Saints in Latin American culture and a symbol of Catholicism.

If you dive deeper into the practices of Santa Muerte's following, you'll find that prayers, altars, and masses are almost identical to those known to any practicing Catholic. It wouldn't even be surprising to find some Santa Muerte followers claiming that worshiping her is a practice of the Catholic Church. Despite this, there is also anger among Santa Muerte followers that the Church has been less than welcoming toward their patron saint since it goes against the history of Latin American Catholicism, where indigenous beliefs and traditions were often mixed naturally with Catholic doctrines. Even the Spanish conquerors were wise enough to leverage the Aztec's veneration of Lady Death and infused that with their Catholic preaching.

On the other hand, Catholic priests have their reasons for denouncing Santa Muerte and opposing her veneration. Cardinal Ravasi, for instance, explains that Jesus defeated death, so worshiping a figure that represents death can be considered blasphemous because her devotees are linked to God's true enemies – Satan and Death. In other words, for them, religion celebrates life while the cult of Santa Muerte embraces death.

Moreover, another reason why the Church has been adamant in its rejection of Santa Muerte is its connection to the LGBTQ communities. Like the State, the Church has always had a say in what people do with their bodies. It has often policed that through religious beliefs and doctrines, which have significantly changed over the years. Consequently, the idea that there is a saint out there for the "deviants" is distressing for the Church since Santa Muerte is more than just that. She's not just a saint for the outlaws but also for those that live outside the Church. She provides solace for them and considers them devout believers, which is a view that the Church has never held in relation to deviants.

In other words, Santa Muerte is an unsanctioned saint who embraces those rejected by the church and approves of them. On the one hand, you have the Church doctrines when it comes to ordaining LGBTQ members, divorcees, and women. On the other, the church of Santa Muerte ordains women, LGBTQ members, and divorced people and outlaws. This has often led many Mexican Catholic bishops to highlight some crimes committed by Santa Muerte followers to claim that those devotees are Satanists. In many ways, the Church's stance against the Santa Muerte cult is not much different from Evangelical and Pentecostal churches, adds Andrew Chesnut, which are all challenges to the

Roman Catholic Church's dominance in Latin America.

Looking at the Church's view from a different angle, the problem with Santa Muerte's sainthood is grounded in personhood and its definition in Catholicism. "The Church canonizes people of flesh and blood who have distinguished themselves by being loving; it does not canonize other facts or other things, and will never canonize holy obedience, poverty, or accountability," says José Luis Chávez Botello. In other words, Santa Muerte's devotees believe that she is the personification of death itself, which rationalizes the Catholic position that she can never be a saint. She is not a person but rather a fact of life or a notion that all humans know - death. This means that she cannot be labeled as saint-like, others of flesh and blood who have risen to that status.

"Without a connection to a particular historical personage, Santa Muerte cannot be canonized within the Catholic faith. As an abstract entity associated with an existential state, she is not qualified as one of the men and women of flesh and blood who show us how to live in faith, in a specific time in which they lived and fled their historic moment," Botello adds. Rafael Romo Muñoz, Archbishop of Tijuana, agrees with that sentiment and says, "The alleged Santa Muerte is not a person, it's an idea. Therefore, we cannot give our assent, our reverence for what is not there. Ours is an encounter with the person as Christ was, the Virgin who was a woman like our own, the apostles, including us, those who are baptized."

Despite the fact that, as we said earlier, many of Santa Muerte's followers claim to be Catholics and find no contradictions in light of the Church's continuous attacks on their faith, some are beginning to declare their dissent and their separation from the Catholic Church. For such persons, praying to other saints and other venerated figures within the Catholic doctrines does no good, and it's Santa Muerte who comes through for them. They believe that Santa Muerte is a powerful force "second only to God." Those Santa Muerte devotees view traditional Catholic teachings in a new light and rework them to create a deeper understanding of religion that suits their new reality.

Whatever the future has in store for the Church of Santa Muerte, it will most likely have nothing to do with the Roman Catholic Church, which has worked hard (and still does) to cut off any ties to the Santa Muerte following. For the Church, it doesn't matter that the association with Santa Muerte is folk and that there are no official ties. It doesn't desire any connection of any kind to the Santa Muerte following, though some Mexican bishops are heavily invested in trying to lure back Santa Muerte devotees into the traditional Catholic faith. Bishop Michael Pfeifer, Diocese of San Angelo, has gone on record and said, "Those who promote the Santa Muerte are trying to pass this off as another type or another form of devotion or religion. It's blasphemy against God. This would become the patron saint, with a quotation mark, patron saint of drug traffickers, and they use it as a religion, a false religion." He has gone on to develop a special ministry for Santa Muerte followers who feel that they are "trapped in a cycle they can't escape from."

However, it can be very interesting for the neutral reader to observe the differences between the Roman Catholic Church and the Santa Muerte Church. Each party has its unique perspective on the matter and is heavily invested in their faith. Whether the Church admits it or not, there are countless similarities between the Bony Lady traditions and Catholic doctrines. Observing those differences and similarities allows us to see how the Church's own set of beliefs and traditions developed over the years and will most likely continue developing. For instance, the Catholic Church's stance toward LGBTQ members has mellowed with the passage of time. It isn't as aggressive and dismissive as it used to be, but it is still not as accepting as Santa Muerte.

Will the Church further develop its traditions and doctrine to keep up with those separating from it to find a more accommodating patron? Time will tell, but in the meantime, observing the spread of the Santa Muerte traditions is quite interesting and eye-opening.

State Oppression

Santa Muerte devotees have often also found themselves at odds with law enforcement. Ever since the Most Holy Death came into the spotlight, she had been a target for state and officials, who often condemned her and at times even persecuted her followers. The relationship between the Mexican government and the Santa Muerte cult has always been complicated, but it got significantly more complicated after the early 2000s when she came to light.

Around 2002, the Traditional Apostolic Catholic Church Mexico-USA created the Sanctuary of Holy Death in Mexico City, which was registered as a religious organization. This naturally caused quite the controversy and drew a lot of heat from both Church and State. Succumbing to the pressure from the Catholic Church and as a way of appeasing his own Catholic voters, Mexico's President Vicente Fox revoked the Sanctuary's status as a religious organization a few years later under the ruse that the Santa Muerte Church did not meet the qualifications of a religion. This decision led to protests across the country, and Santa Muerte was under the spotlight once again.

State hostility toward Santa Muerte and her followers only increased in the subsequent years, with the government regularly harassing followers and destroying shrines. More Mexican presidents condemned the cult following, and President Felipe

Calderon even declared the Bony Lady "an enemy of the Mexican State." He didn't stop there either. During his term, Calderon ordered the army to bulldoze many Santa Muerte shrines along the US-Mexico borders in a move not much different from what the Spanish conquerors used to do. This was nothing short of a desecration of a holy worship site that was quite odd and caused many to wonder what Santa Muerte and her followers did to warrant such aggression and hatred.

On the other hand, the Mexican government's stance toward Santa Muerte has always been that she is a threat to national security. For many officials in the Mexican government, Santa Muerte is closely associated with the drug cartels, with whom they have had an ongoing and very long war. In other words, the State believes that Santa Muerte is responsible for and associated with violence, crime, and much of the illegal activity in the country. They have no problem hunting her cult down for it. History shows that Santa Muerte has been involved in several violent crimes over the decades in one way or the other.

Adolfo de Jesús Constanzo was a Cuban-American serial killer, cult leader, and drug lord.

He was the head of a notorious drug trafficking and occult cult/gang in the area of Matamoros. Under his commands, the cult committed several ritualistic murders of a particularly obscene nature in the 1980s. It is said that he invoked Santa Muerte during his final moments. Another altar was found in Juana Barraza's home, one of Mexico's worst serial killers responsible for the death of almost 40 victims. These are just a few examples of many where notorious criminals declared their association with Santa Muerte, which is one of the reasons why the State always had her in their crosshairs.

It wasn't just Mexico's government that feared Santa Muerte. There have been reports commissioned by the US Department of Defense analyzing Saint Death's connection to drug trafficking and violent crimes. She was also featured more than once in FBI bulletins, emphasizing her connection to Mexico's drug lords. An FBI report by Robert J. Bunker, an Epochal Warfare Studies scholar, said, "Officer performance and safety issues, primarily those of an emotional or mental nature, need consideration during investigations of crime scenes involving Santa Muerte altars and ritualistic activities, even benign ones.... For specialized federal assistance, the FBI can provide training in the management of death investigations and spirituality."

Yet, despite all of the above and Santa Muerte's association with crime, many agree that it would be nonsensical to consider that all of those who follow her are criminals. Millions of Saint Death's devotees are just ordinary citizens with no association to crime, organized or otherwise. There are even plenty of cops who believe in and pray to her, asking for her protection and help when hunting drug lords and criminals. Criminals have different faiths and beliefs, but it's the Santa Muerte cult that is often targeted.

It wouldn't be unreasonable to believe that the Mexican and US governments fear Santa Muerte for reasons beyond her alleged association with crime and criminals. There is more to the story than that. Santa Muerte is a saint for the disenfranchised and those living on the fringes of society, abandoned by their governments, and that alone is enough reason for any State to fear her. "This rise in deviant spirituality has not come as a surprise. Mexico still contains a significant population of persons living in poverty and feeling disenfranchised by a government system perceived as being based on patron-client relationships and the influence of wealthy ruling families. This underclass produces a disproportionate amount of unsanctioned (folk) saint worshipers—though only a small percentage of them end up as killers for gangs and cartels," Bunker adds.

The undeniable fact is many people have devoted themselves to Santa Muerte and believe that she is their savior. These people feel that the government and the Church have failed them, so they turned to an all-powerful folk saint to help and guide them. Neither the Church nor the government could deliver these people from poverty, but maybe Santa Muerte could, they believe. This is why the State feels threatened by the cult of Santa Muerte. The state of political – and religious – despair in a country like Mexico is widespread and dangerous to the stability and sustainability of any government. Santa Muerte is the spirit of resistance to many of those people rejected by society and disempowered by the state, which is enough to scare any government.

Another way to look at it from a psychological point of view is that Saint Death empowers her followers in a way no other saint has or can. She is death itself, and not only does she protect her followers from death, but she also understands those who live close to it every day of their lives due to poverty and misfortune – from the extremely poor to the transgender sex workers. And thus, by embracing Santa Muerte, her devotees rise against and negate death's power itself, which means they are a danger and a threat to the social norms and the order established to keep them where they are: poor, shunned, and desperate. With Saint Death, they have much less to fear if they can conquer death itself.

If you think about it, the State's response and concern about Santa Muerte is a mere reflection of its stance toward the majority of her devotees: sex workers, undocumented migrants, and lower social classes. These people have been welcomed by neither Church nor State, and they pose a threat to nationalist ideals and the desire to police people's bodies. On the other hand, Saint Death crossed borders and boundaries to stand up for all the oppressed irrespective of their backgrounds. She accepts the poor and marginalized without discrimination, and, in the eyes of the government, that is a dangerous folk saint for the people to have.

Part of the animosity toward Santa Muerte, whether by State or Church, has been fueled by sensationalist media coverage that often paints her as a vile figure whose followers make for an evil cult. The focus in the media when it comes to Saint Death is often on the criminals and illegal activities associated with her rather than trying to explore why a figure of death has gained this much popularity in the country in such a short time. However, Santa Muerte's followers are only increasing in number, despite the best efforts of the State and Church.

Another major reason why both the US and Mexican governments are harsh towards Santa Muerte's devotees is the fact that the Bony Lady is highly present along the borders between the two countries. It's quite likely that officials in the US believe that Santa Muerte is empowering and encouraging people to illegally cross the borders, making the Bony Lady a permanent enemy. The US-

Mexico border is one of the most militarized border zones in the world, which is ironic considering the fact that both countries are allies. People die by the thousands crossing the borders, and the last thing the US government wants is controversy, which may explain the general animosity toward Santa Muerte. On the other hand, with this much death surrounding the border area, it's not surprising that Santa Muerte is an important part of the lives of the many who try to cross to the other side.

Chapter Four:

The Faith

We've touched earlier on the many similarities between the Santa Muerte church and Catholicism, folk Catholicism to be specific. Saint Death's devotees have drawn a lot of influence from traditional Catholic practices and infused it with their devotion and reverence to Santa Muerte. In Catholicism, a saint will become revered and popular among worshipers who will then make a shrine or an altar in their name. Then, followers would flock to those shrines and altars to pray to the saints and ask them for favors, healing, or guidance. This is similarly done with folk saints like Santa Muerte, who the church has not canonized. However, despite drawing many influences from Catholicism, the followers of Santa Muerte have also drawn practices from other influences such as western medicine, Santería, spiritualism, and even new age concepts concerning spiritual energy and healing. With folk saints, devotees believe that a figure like

Santa Muerte can lift a curse, help them heal from a terrible illness, find good fortune, get a job, and much more.

Practices and Beliefs

The practices of Santa Muerte devotees are also quite similar to Catholicism. They pray with rosaries, put apples, candles, cigars, alcohol, and other items as offerings on her altars, and even go on pilgrimages. In some places, you can expect to find some magical practices associated with the Santa Muerte following, drawn from the many influences listed above.

In the Christian faith, devotees request a miracle by making a vow or a promise, seeking divine intervention to fix a problem in their lives. They make a request to the saint in exchange for an offering. The same is done with Santa Muerte, as with any saint, folk, or canonized. Yet, despite the similarity, the relationship Saint Death has with her devotees is more potent since they believe her to be the most powerful miracle worker, her powers binding and her will fierce. Moreover, there is more fear involved when it comes to deals with Santa

Muerte. Her devotees know her to be ruthless with her punishment for those who break their deals. This isn't the case with canonized saints or even many of the ordinary folk saints.

To sum up, Santa Muerte's followers perform rituals, pray, and make pilgrimages to request that she activate her superpowers in their favor. But even with this strong variation on Catholicism, the rituals are quite similar. Santa Muerte's followers hold masses, novenas, and prayers in her name that have the traditional catholic form, but in a different context. This makes it easier for her devotees to attract new followers. Many of the practices by the church of Santa Muerte are already ingrained in many Mexicans who practice folk Catholicism, which makes the Santa Muerte rituals all the more familiar.

Altars play a very important role in the devotion to Santa Muerte. While they were almost all private in the past, many are now public as her cult has spread. The alter's importance is that it serves as a portal to communicate with the Bony Lady herself and a way to honor her and offer her offerings. Altars for Santa Muerte vary in size and decoration.

Some are simply a small statue for her surrounded by votive candles, while others are more elaborate and occupy sacred spaces with much attention given to every detail of the space.

Unlike the use of altars dedicated to official saints, with Santa Muerte, things are more flexible. Her rituals are colorful and full of life, despite being the representation of death. With scarce cult organization and the absence of official doctrines, Santa Muerte's followers are often free to reach out to her however they please. Still, despite this flexibility, many of her serious devotees prefer to honor Santa Muerte through a series of well-planned prayers and rituals.

One of the most famous rituals in her name was established by the woman behind the current popularity of Saint Death, Doña Queta. The rosary (el Rosario) is one of the cult's most practiced collective rituals, and it's also a variation of the Catholic prayers to the Virgin. The first rosary was held at Doña Queta's public shrine in 2002, and from there, the practice spread out across Mexico and the United States. There even used to be a monthly service at Doña Queta's shrine, which often attracted many people from all over the country and beyond.

There are plenty of other altars across the country where devotees come to leave red apples, tobacco, flowers, candles, and alcohol as offerings for Saint Death, hoping she can cure their pains and help with their trouble. They are often warned not to make any promises to Santa Muerte that they cannot keep lest they incur her wrath. You can find variations in the way of worshipping Santa Muerte across the country, but there are some basics that any devotee has to adhere to. She has to be given the respect she's due and the reverence worthy of a saint that is always working under the guidance and leadership of God.

Despite many Catholic bishops and priests in Mexico claiming that the worship of Santa Muerte borders on Satanism, her devotees don't really pay much attention to that and often view her in the light of God. They have figurines for her in their homes, to which they speak, pray, and show reverence. They celebrate her presence and dress her in colorful outfits, making Saint Death a part of their daily lives, for she is the one who will help them with their daily struggles.

Votive Candle Rituals

One of the most popular practices for Santa Muerte followers is petitioning and praying to her using votive candles, which will often have different colors depending on the kind of need you have for her. Those candles mean different things to different people, and they are used in a variety of rituals and practices. You can find them in most herbal shops and markets in Mexico, along with many Santa Muerte objects. Those candles usually have an image of her in her robe drawn on the front, holding a scythe and/or any of the other objects mentioned earlier. On the backs of these votive candles, you can find prayers that correspond to the color of the candle and its meaning. In some cases, the candle might have additional prayer cards to guide the devotees.

The color-coding of the candles is very important, and its symbolism is rooted in devotion to and reverence for Santa Muerte. While there are many color options, there are three main ones: red, black, and white. If you wish to petition Santa

Muerte and ask her for a favor, you put the candle on the altar, your particular need determining the color, and you pray to her. Some followers keep a variety of Santa Muerte votive candles in different colors, while others prefer to focus on just one aspect of her powers. In general, Santa Muerte is invoked for matters of health, love, justice, money, and others.

Red candles, for example, symbolize love and passion, and you use those if you want to attract love or preserve an existing relationship with someone you care about. It can also be used in other matters of the heart, like ending bad or toxic relationships. Some trace the origins of red candles all the way back to the colonial times in Mexico and the love magic practiced in that era, which was believed to have been brought from Europe. It shouldn't come as a surprise that one of the more popular prayers for Santa Muerte has to do with love and involves the use of red candles, as she is believed to be a force of love and a doer of miracles. Love rituals often include other components to make the spells potent enough, such as cinnamon for prosperity, red roses for passion, and rose water.

Brown candles are used to attract wisdom and enlightenment for those in leadership positions or just seeking an enlightened answer to a difficult dilemma. White candles are for gratitude, and they can also be used to consecrate other objects. Santa Muerte white votive candles are some of the most popular since they symbolize purity and protection. On the other hand, gold candles are used to attract wealth and money for those who are facing financial difficulties. Purple candles are used by those seeking spiritual and/or physical healing from some ailment, and they are very popular in places where healthcare isn't exactly accessible to all. Green candles are used for those seeking justice and are looking for equality in the eyes of the law.

It's black candles, though, that have often been a source of controversy. While they are used for protection, they are also used for vengeance, and they have been associated with black magic. When a Santa Muerte devotee lights a black votive candle, they implore her for protection or vengeance. But even for protection purposes, it was used by drug traffickers and criminals to ask Santa Muerte for protection as they smuggled shipments of drugs across borders or embarked on other illegal endeavors. Drug traffickers also used black votive candles for protection against rival gangs and to ensure harm to their adversaries, be they cops or rival gang members.

It was quite frequent in many drug raids that law enforcement would find black candles in the houses of drug traffickers and gang members, which sort of gave a bad reputation to Santa Muerte's black votive candles above all. The media attention on Santa Muerte's black candles found on altars of notorious criminals also contributed to these ones being the least available and popular. This is why you'll hardly find any black votive candles being sold at local shops and markets, and those who happen to obtain them often keep them in the privacy of their homes. Despite their darker uses, black votive candles can be used for good in the right hands and for purposes such as protecting yourself from dark energy and reversing evil spells.

Votive candles can be found in other colors like blue, which are popular among students and used for insight and gaining clarity. Yellow votive candles are used to ask for Santa Muerte's help in overcoming addiction. These colors can be found in plenty of altars for Saint Death across Mexico and the United States, where people use them to ask for Santa Muerte's help in their daily struggles. They will vary from one ritual to the other, but the concept remains the same: those candles serve to establish a connection to Saint Death for a specific purpose depending on the color chosen. And as you can see, there is a color for every possible purpose, from love to hatred and vengeance, and everything in between.

Conclusion

To examine Santa Muerte's incredible influence on millions of lives, you have to step back and look at the bigger picture. Within just twenty years, Saint Death's cult went on from being almost un-known to being a refuge for millions of lost souls who didn't have anyone to believe in. This meteoric rise has stirred a lot of controversies and garnered a lot of attention, but the fact remains: the Santa Muerte following is one of the fastest-growing in the world, with millions of devotees praying to her and holding rituals in her name.

Despite negative media coverage, State opposition, and Church condemnation, the cult is only growing bigger and being adopted by people across borders far beyond Mexico. The association of Santa Muerte with crime and illegal activities has not swayed millions from embracing her as their savior and protector, looking beyond the fact that she is actually Saint Death. To them, she injects enough death into their lives to protect them from death and pain. By taking a deep look into history, you will find the connection between Santa Muerte and other Aztec figures or any of the other civilizations that may have given birth to the Santa Muerte we know today. This, however, wouldn't really matter to any of her followers. They know her in her current form, a folk saint who will answer their prayers and keep them safe in a world that doesn't care about them.

Santa Muerte won't judge people coming to her for help, and she won't condemn them for their past mistakes or their intentions to do anything, albeit slightly illegal. She doesn't care about her followers' color, creed, sex, orientation, or class, so long as they keep their promises and venerate her. For that reason alone, she will never stop meaning as much to those who have been constantly told that they are not good enough or that they don't deserve a second chance. Santa Muerte may not snap someone out of poverty, but she gives them hope that it is not impossible, which is more than what any other saint had given them. Santa Muerte gives people hope and comfort in knowing that they are not alone, and for that, they will never stop loving her.

Despite the similarities between the Santa Muerte and Catholicism rituals, chances are, the Church will always oppose the Bony Lady. To the Church, she is death, which Jesus vanquished in his resurrection. Still, it is hoped that the Church can eventually find some common ground and a way to embrace the millions that follow Santa Muerte, many of whom are still practicing Catholics who do not wish to separate themselves from the Church. Worshiping and praying Santa Muerte does not preclude them from being Catholics and believing in God. They simply find Santa Muerte to be a powerful folk saint who has answered their problems.

If you're ever in Mexico or along with the border cities in the US, keep an open mind when you see a Santa Muerte shrine. Look beyond the bony skeleton and the strange offering at her shrine. You'll find that she is a figure that brings hope to many people who are in desperate need of it. Who knows, maybe one day you'll say a prayer to Santa Muerte and find that what you prayed for came to be because Saint Death's power spans life and death. If anyone can make wishes come true, it's her.

References

Carey, L. (2017, December 9). Everything you need to know about Santa Muerte. Retrieved from Theculturetrip.com website: https://theculturetrip.com/north-america/mexico/articles/everything-you-need-to-know-about-santa-muerte/

David, V. A. P. (2013, November 8). The last enemy to be defeated is death – Clarification on the Catholic Church's rejection of Santa Muerte. Retrieved from Skeletonsaint.com website: https://skeletonsaint.com/2013/11/08/the-last-enemy/

Dimuro, G. (2018, December 9). Santa Muerte: The saint of death that the Vatican tried to shut down. Retrieved from Allthatsinteresting.com website: https://allthatsinteresting.com/santa-muerte

Dorling, S. (2020, September 27). Top 25 gods of death, destruction, and the underworld. Retrieved from Thepopularlist.com website: https://

thepopularlist.com/gods-of-death-destruction-underworld/

Farrow, M. (2017, November 4). Have you heard of Saint Death? Don't pray to her. Retrieved from Catholic News Agency website: https://www.catholicnewsagency.com/news/34832/have-you-heard-of-saint-death-dont-pray-to-her

Graham, J. (n.d.). The worship of Santa Muerte – The Manitoban. Retrieved from Themanitoban.com website: https://www.themanitoban.com/2010/03/the-worship-of-santa-muerte/989/

Lorentzen, L. A. (n.d.). Santa Muerte: Saint of the dispossessed, enemy of church and state. Retrieved from Hemisphericinstitute.org website: https://hemisphericinstitute.org/en/emisferica-13-1-states-of-devotion/13-1-essays/santa-muerte-saint-of-the-dispossessed-enemy-of-church-and-state.html

Myth of Mictecacihuatl- Aztec goddess of the dead. (2020, November 6). Retrieved from Mangopublishinggroup.com website: https://mangopublishinggroup.com/myth-of-mictecacihuatl-aztec-goddess-of-the-dead/

Portebois, X. (2017). Santa Muerte. Realities.

The Editors of Encyclopedia Britannica. (2020). Mictlantecuhtli. In Encyclopedia Britannica.

Tucker, D. (2017, November 1). Santa Muerte: The rise of Mexico's death "saint." BBC. Retrieved from https://www.bbc.com/news/world-latin-america-41804243

Woody, C. (2016, March 17). Saint Death: The secretive and sinister "cult" challenging the power of the Catholic Church. Business Insider. Retrieved from https://www.businessinsider.com/what-is-santa-muerte-2016-3

(N.d.). Retrieved from Jstor.org website: https://daily.jstor.org/who-is-santa-muerte